HAL•LEONARD
INSTRUMENTAL
PLAY-ALONG

AUDIO ACCESS INCLUDED

PLAYBACK+
ed • Pitch • Balance • Loop

VIOLIN

Jazz Classics

T0061432

Audio arrangements by Peter Deneff

To access audio visit:
www.halleonard.com/mylibrary

Enter Code
3770-8575-4426-6280

ISBN 978-1-4950-4754-1

7777 W. BLUEMOUND RD. P.O. BOX 13819 MILWAUKEE, WI 53213

For all works contained herein:
Unauthorized copying, arranging, adapting, recording, Internet posting, public performance,
or other distribution of the printed or recorded music in this publication is an infringement of copyright.
Infringers are liable under the law.

Visit Hal Leonard Online at
www.halleonard.com

DOXY

VIOLIN

By SONNY ROLLINS

Copyright © 1963 Prestige Music c/o The Bicycle Music Company
Copyright Renewed
International Copyright Secured   All Rights Reserved

D.S. al Coda
(with repeat)

IN WALKED BUD

VIOLIN

By THELONIOUS MONK

Copyright © 1948 (Renewed) by Embassy Music Corporation (BMI)
International Copyright Secured   All Rights Reserved
Reprinted by Permission

IN YOUR OWN SWEET WAY

Violin

By DAVE BRUBECK

Copyright © 1955, 1956 by Derry Music Co.
Copyright Renewed
Sole Selling Agent: Shawnee Press, Inc.
International Copyright Secured   All Rights Reserved
Reprinted by Permission

MERCY, MERCY, MERCY

VIOLIN

Composed by JOSEF ZAWINUL

Copyright © 1966 Zawinul Enterprises LLC
Copyright Renewed
All Rights Administered by Songs Of Kobalt Music Publishing
All Rights Reserved   Used by Permission

NARDIS

Violin

By MILES DAVIS

Copyright © 1959 Jazz Horn Music Corporation
Copyright Renewed
All Rights Administered by Songs Of Kobalt Music Publishing
All Rights Reserved   Used by Permission

ON GREEN DOLPHIN STREET

Violin

Lyrics by NED WASHINGTON
Music by BRONISLAU KAPER

© 1947 (Renewed) Catharine Hinen Music, Patti Washington Music and Primary Wave Songs
All Rights for Catharine Hinen Music Controlled by Shapiro, Bernstein & Co., Inc.
All Rights for Primary Wave Songs Controlled by EMI April Music Inc. (Publishing) and Alfred Music (Print)
All Rights Reserved   Used by Permission

REUNION BLUES

VIOLIN

By MILT JACKSON

Copyright © 1962 (Renewed 1990) by MJQ Music, Inc.
All Rights Administered by Hal Leonard - Milwin Music Corp.
International Copyright Secured   All Rights Reserved

STOLEN MOMENTS

VIOLIN

Words and Music by
OLIVER NELSON

Copyright © 1962, 1965 by Noslen Music Co. LLC
Copyright Renewed
All Rights for the World Administered by Alameda Music Company
International Copyright Secured   All Rights Reserved
Used by Permission

ST. THOMAS

VIOLIN

By SONNY ROLLINS

Copyright © 1963 Prestige Music c/o The Bicycle Music Company
Copyright Renewed
International Copyright Secured   All Rights Reserved

D.S. al Coda
(with repeat)

SCRAPPLE FROM THE APPLE

VIOLIN

By CHARLIE PARKER

Copyright © 1957 (Renewed 1985) Atlantic Music Corp.
International Copyright Secured   All Rights Reserved

SIDEWINDER

VIOLIN

By Lee Morgan

Copyright © 1959 (Renewed) Conrad Music (BMI)
U.S. Rights owned by Arc/Conrad Music LLC (Administered by BMG Rights Management (US) LLC)
International Copyright Secured   All Rights Reserved

TAKE FIVE

VIOLIN

By PAUL DESMOND

small notes optional

© 1960 (Renewed 1988) Desmond Music Company
All Rights outside the USA Controlled by Derry Music Company
International Copyright Secured   All Rights Reserved

HAL•LEONARD INSTRUMENTAL PLAY-ALONG

Your favorite songs are arranged just for solo instrumentalists with this outstanding series. Each book includes a great full-accompaniment play-along audio so you can sound just like a pro! Check out **www.halleonard.com** to see all the titles available.

The Beatles

All You Need Is Love • Blackbird • Day Tripper • Eleanor Rigby • Get Back • Here, There and Everywhere • Hey Jude • I Will • Let It Be • Lucy in the Sky with Diamonds • Ob-La-Di, Ob-La-Da • Penny Lane • Something • Ticket to Ride • Yesterday.

_____00225330	Flute	$14.99
_____00225331	Clarinet	$14.99
_____00225332	Alto Sax	$14.99
_____00225333	Tenor Sax	$14.99
_____00225334	Trumpet	$14.99
_____00225335	Horn	$14.99
_____00225336	Trombone	$14.99
_____00225337	Violin	$14.99
_____00225338	Viola	$14.99
_____00225339	Cello	$14.99

Chart Hits

All About That Bass • All of Me • Happy • Radioactive • Roar • Say Something • Shake It Off • A Sky Full of Stars • Someone like You • Stay with Me • Thinking Out Loud • Uptown Funk.

_____00146207	Flute	$12.99
_____00146208	Clarinet	$12.99
_____00146209	Alto Sax	$12.99
_____00146210	Tenor Sax	$12.99
_____00146211	Trumpet	$12.99
_____00146212	Horn	$12.99
_____00146213	Trombone	$12.99
_____00146214	Violin	$12.99
_____00146215	Viola	$12.99
_____00146216	Cello	$12.99

Coldplay

Clocks • Every Teardrop Is a Waterfall • Fix You • In My Place • Lost! • Paradise • The Scientist • Speed of Sound • Trouble • Violet Hill • Viva La Vida • Yellow.

_____00103337	Flute	$12.99
_____00103338	Clarinet	$12.99
_____00103339	Alto Sax	$12.99
_____00103340	Tenor Sax	$12.99
_____00103341	Trumpet	$12.99
_____00103342	Horn	$12.99
_____00103343	Trombone	$12.99
_____00103344	Violin	$12.99
_____00103345	Viola	$12.99
_____00103346	Cello	$12.99

Disney Greats

Arabian Nights • Hawaiian Roller Coaster Ride • It's a Small World • Look Through My Eyes • Yo Ho (A Pirate's Life for Me) • and more.

_____00841934	Flute	$12.99
_____00841935	Clarinet	$12.99
_____00841936	Alto Sax	$12.99
_____00841937	Tenor Sax	$12.95
_____00841938	Trumpet	$12.99
_____00841939	Horn	$12.99
_____00841940	Trombone	$12.95
_____00841941	Violin	$12.99
_____00841942	Viola	$12.99
_____00841943	Cello	$12.99
_____00842078	Oboe	$12.99

Great Themes

Bella's Lullaby • Chariots of Fire • Get Smart • Hawaii Five-O Theme • I Love Lucy • The Odd Couple • Spanish Flea • and more.

_____00842468	Flute	$12.99
_____00842469	Clarinet	$12.99
_____00842470	Alto Sax	$12.99
_____00842471	Tenor Sax	$12.99
_____00842472	Trumpet	$12.99
_____00842473	Horn	$12.99
_____00842474	Trombone	$12.99
_____00842475	Violin	$12.99
_____00842476	Viola	$12.99
_____00842477	Cello	$12.99

Popular Hits

Breakeven • Fireflies • Halo • Hey, Soul Sister • I Gotta Feeling • I'm Yours • Need You Now • Poker Face • Viva La Vida • You Belong with Me • and more.

_____00842511	Flute	$12.99
_____00842512	Clarinet	$12.99
_____00842513	Alto Sax	$12.99
_____00842514	Tenor Sax	$12.99
_____00842515	Trumpet	$12.99
_____00842516	Horn	$12.99
_____00842517	Trombone	$12.99
_____00842518	Violin	$12.99
_____00842519	Viola	$12.99
_____00842520	Cello	$12.99

Songs from Frozen, Tangled and Enchanted

Do You Want to Build a Snowman? • For the First Time in Forever • Happy Working Song • I See the Light • In Summer • Let It Go • Mother Knows Best • That's How You Know • True Love's First Kiss • When Will My Life Begin • and more.

_____00126921	Flute	$14.99
_____00126922	Clarinet	$14.99
_____00126923	Alto Sax	$14.99
_____00126924	Tenor Sax	$14.99
_____00126925	Trumpet	$14.99
_____00126926	Horn	$14.99
_____00126927	Trombone	$14.99
_____00126928	Violin	$14.99
_____00126929	Viola	$14.99
_____00126930	Cello	$14.99

Top Hits

Adventure of a Lifetime • Budapest • Die a Happy Man • Ex's & Oh's • Fight Song • Hello • Let It Go • Love Yourself • One Call Away • Pillowtalk • Stitches • Writing's on the Wall.

_____00171073	Flute	$12.99
_____00171074	Clarinet	$12.99
_____00171075	Alto Sax	$12.99
_____00171106	Tenor Sax	$12.99
_____00171107	Trumpet	$12.99
_____00171108	Horn	$12.99
_____00171109	Trombone	$12.99
_____00171110	Violin	$12.99
_____00171111	Viola	$12.99
_____00171112	Cello	$12.99

Wicked

As Long As You're Mine • Dancing Through Life • Defying Gravity • For Good • I'm Not That Girl • Popular • The Wizard and I • and more.

_____00842236	Flute	$12.99
_____00842237	Clarinet	$12.99
_____00842238	Alto Saxophone	$11.95
_____00842239	Tenor Saxophone	$11.95
_____00842240	Trumpet	$11.99
_____00842241	Horn	$11.95
_____00842242	Trombone	$12.99
_____00842243	Violin	$11.99
_____00842244	Viola	$12.99
_____00842245	Cello	$12.99

Prices, contents, and availability subject to change without notice.
Disney characters and artwork © Disney Enterprises, Inc.

HAL•LEONARD®

0617